Lacolorfu

Cozy Autumn
Relaxing, Bold and Easy
Coloring Book

Get Cozy!

Relax, unwind, and let your creativity flow with 40 bold & easy coloring pages, perfect for adults, teens, and kids.

Before You Start

To keep our book affordable, we chose to use regular white paper. As a result, some alcohol markers or other wet media might bleed through the pages. To prevent this, place one or two sheets of thick paper behind the coloring page before you begin.

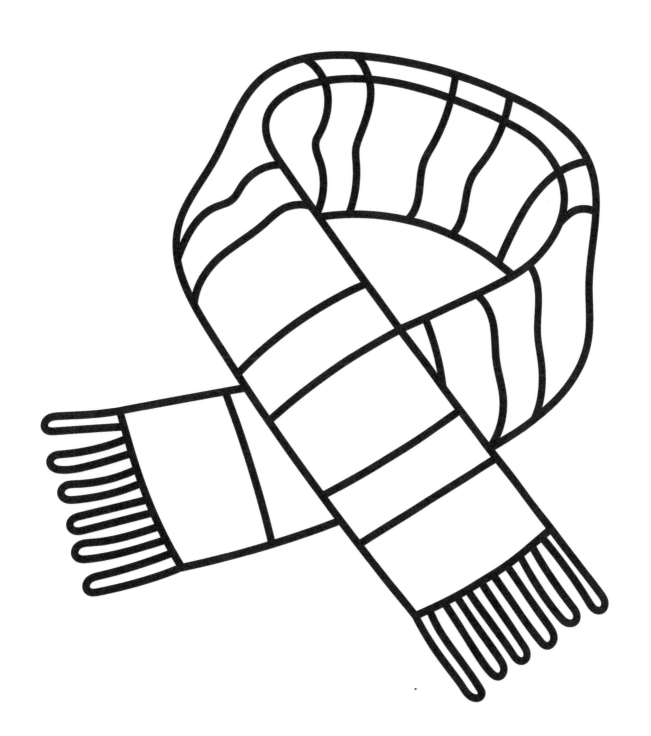

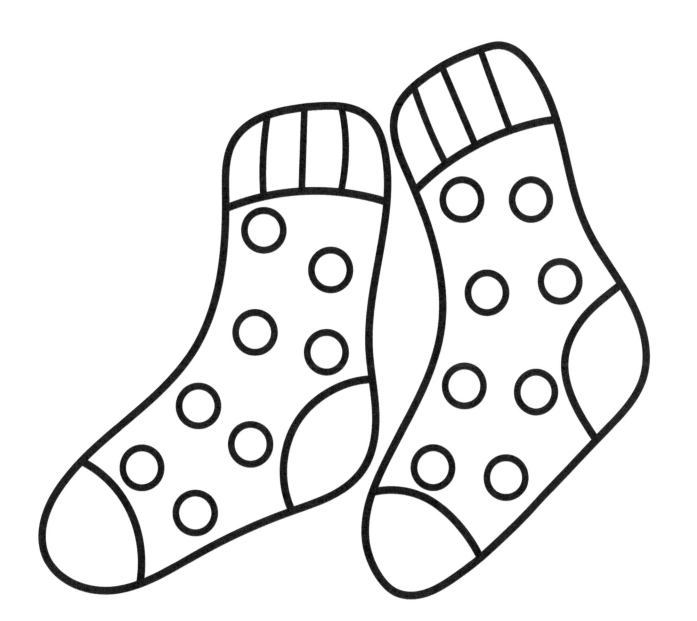

Made in United States
Troutdale, OR
10/28/2024